Why do Bees Buzz?

FOX EYE
PUBLISHING

Why do bees buzz?

Because they flap their
little wings so very fast that
they make a buzzing sound.

Why do they flap their wings so fast?

Because they have
to fly to every flower
in the garden.

Why do they have to fly to every flower?

Because they need to collect the flower's pollen and nectar.

Why do they need to collect the flower's pollen and nectar?

So they can turn it into
honey inside their Beehive.

Why do they turn it into honey?

So their babies have something to eat ...

... and we can have some
delicious honey sandwiches
for our tea.

Let's find out about Bees

Turn the page over to discover the answers to these questions.

How many flowers can a bee visit each day?

How fast can honey bees fly?

How fast do bees beat their wings?

Do all honey bees collect pollen and nectar from flowers?

How much honey can each honey bee make?

How many honey bees can live in a hive?

Let's find out about Bees

The answers are...

Bees can visit up to 2000 flowers a day.

Bees can fly at speeds up to 25 kilometres per hour.

11,400 times a minute. That's 190 times a second!

Only Worker bees visit the flowers. In a hive there is a Queen bee. She lays all the bee eggs, and Drone Bees, that help Queen bees make eggs.

I am a Honey Bee.

About one twelfth of a teaspoon.

Between 20,000 - 60,000 Honey bees live in a single colony. Bumble bees live in much smaller colonies.

I am a White - tailed Bumblebee.

Bzzz

How to use this book

You can read this book with one child or a group of children.

The book can be used to begin a discussion around complex questions such as learning why bees buzz.

The book is also a reading aid, with enlarged and repeated words to help children to develop their reading skills.

How to read the story

Before beginning the story, ensure that the children you are reading to are relaxed and focused.

Take time to look at the enlarged words and the illustrations, and discuss what this book might be about before reading the story.

New words can be tricky for young children to approach.

Sounding them out first, slowly and repeatedly, can help children to learn the words and become familiar with them.

Did you spot the Tardigrade hiding in this book?

First published in 2023 by Fox Eye Publishing
Unit 31, Vulcan House Business Centre,
Vulcan Road, Leicester, LE5 3EF
www.foxeyepublishing.com

Written and illustrated by Simon Couchman

ISBN 978-1-80445-350-6

A catalogue record for this book is available from the British Library.

Printed in China

Titles in the Series

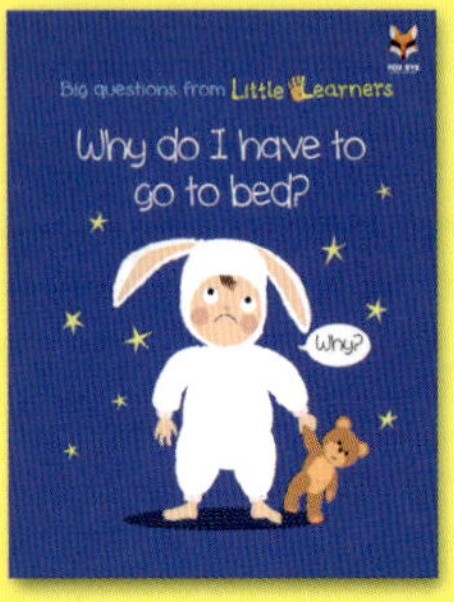

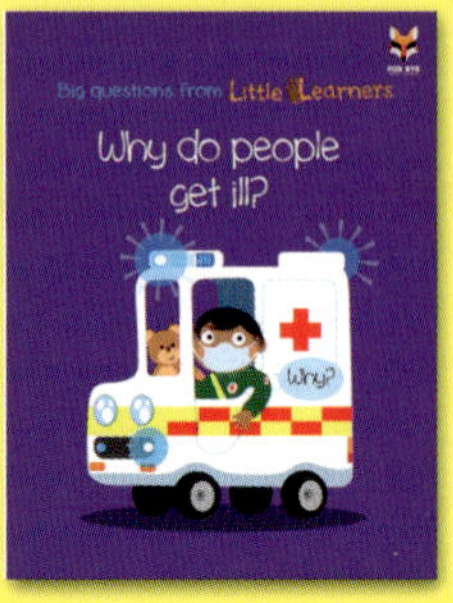

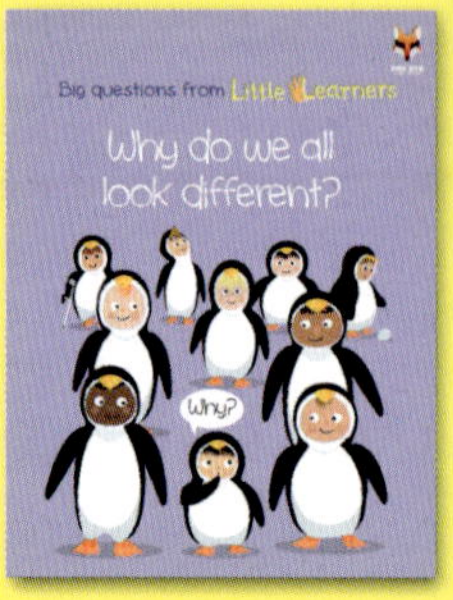

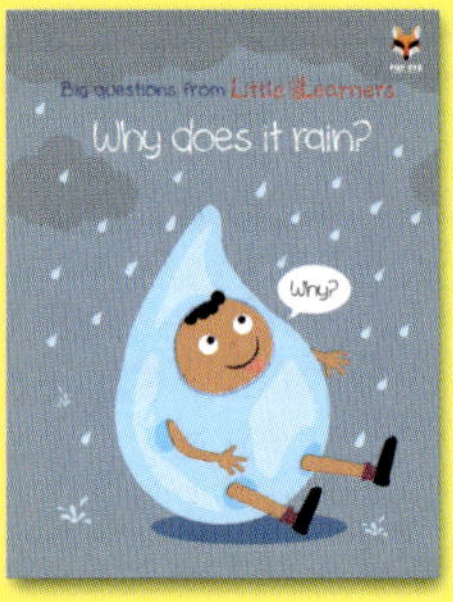

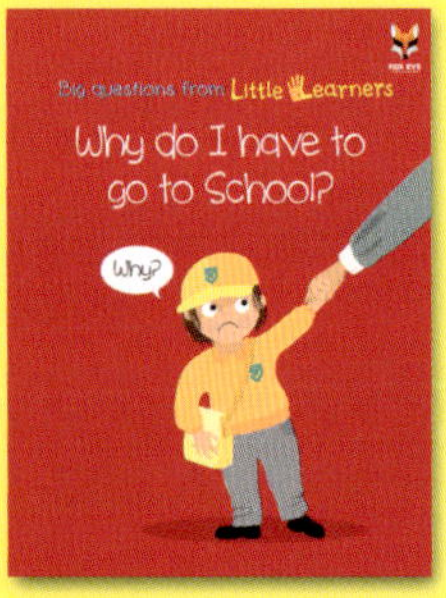